Charles Warren Stoddard

**A Trip to Hawaii**

Charles Warren Stoddard

**A Trip to Hawaii**

ISBN/EAN: 9783337148348

Printed in Europe, USA, Canada, Australia, Japan

Cover: Foto ©Andreas Hilbeck / pixelio.de

More available books at **www.hansebooks.com**

A Trip to Hawaii.          Forbes Co., Boston.

HER MAJESTY QUEEN LILIUOKALANI.

A Trip to Hawaii     *Forbes Co., Boston.*

H.R.H. PRINCESS KAIULANI—HEIR PRESUMPTIVE.

# A ✤ Trip ✤ to ✤ Hawaii:

BY

CHARLES WARREN STODDARD.

WITH

DESCRIPTIVE INTRODUCTION.

New Edition.

ISSUED BY
PASSENGER DEPARTMENT
OCEANIC STEAMSHIP CO.
SAN FRANCISCO
1892.

DIAMOND HEAD.

# ILLUSTRATIONS.

———◆◆◆———

|  | FACING PAGE. |
|---|---|
| Avenue of Royal Palms—Honolulu, | 29 |
| Cocoanut Island—Hilo, | 40 |
| Diamond Head, | 3 |
| Hanapepa Falls, | 20 |
| Hilo Beach, | 25 |
| Honolii Gulch, | 37 |
| Hula Girls, | 32 |
| Kapiolani—Queen Dowager, | v |
| H. R. H. Princess Kaiulani—Heir Presumptive, | *Frontispiece.* |
| Kalakaua—late King of the Hawaiian Islands, | " |
| Her Majesty Queen Liliokalani, | " |
| Lauhala and Cocoanut Grove, | 48 |
| Lava Flow—Near Hilo, | 45 |
| Map of Hawaiian Islands, | iv |
| Oceanic S. S. Co's S. S. Mariposa, | vii |
| Wailua Falls—Kauai, | xii |

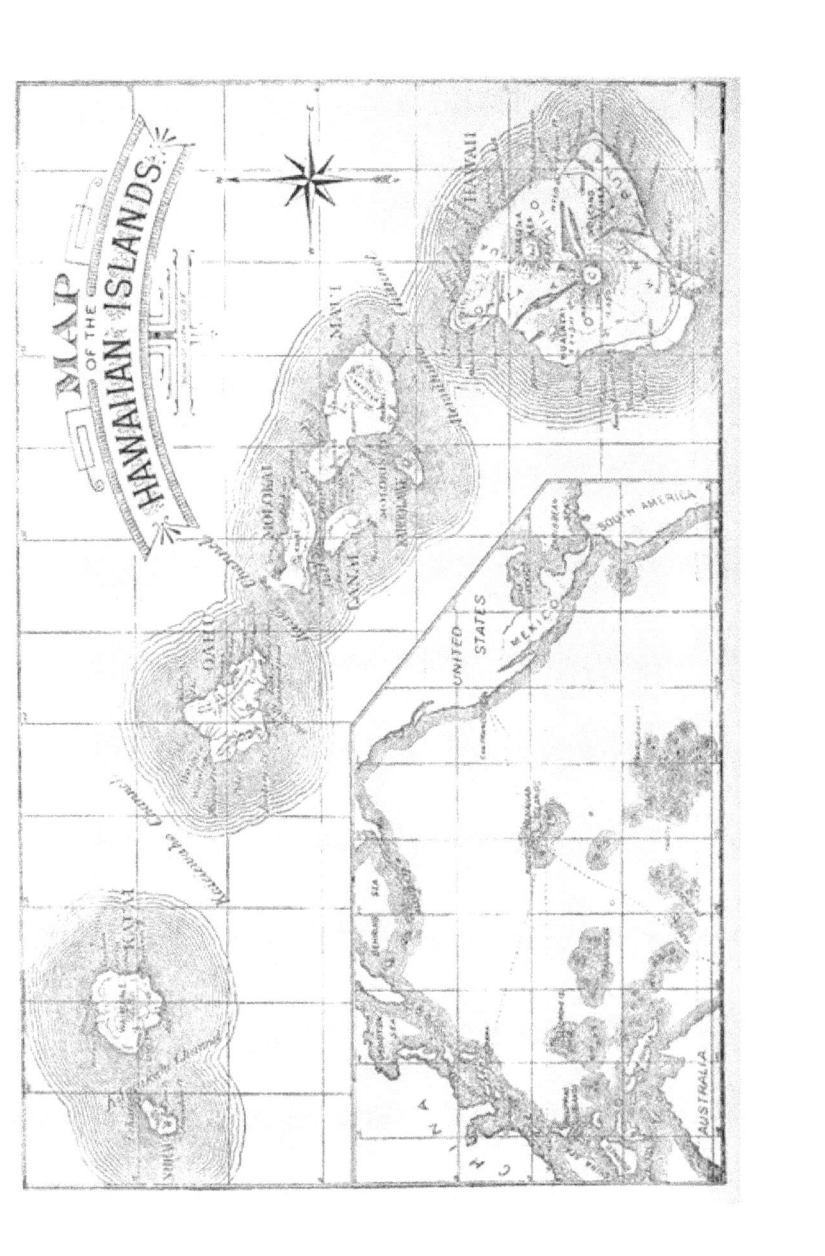

# A TRIP TO HAWAII.

### INTRODUCTORY.

— ●✦● —

A TRIP to the Hawaiian Islands from San Francisco in one of the Oceanic Company's United States and Royal Mail steamships, is perhaps, the most enjoyable in the whole possible range of sea excursions. The distance, 2100 miles, is invariably covered by these superb vessels in seven days. A three thousand ton steamship, fitted with every modern convenience, and capable of running sixteen knots an hour, sails twice a month from the Oceanic Company's Wharf, foot of Folsom street, San Francisco, for Honolulu, and returns at similar stated intervals, thus giving practically a fortnightly steamer service between the Pacific Coast and the Hawaiian Islands.

In addition to the local service, the Australian Mail steamer sails every fourth week from the Oceanic Company's wharf for Auckland and Sydney, calling at Honolulu *en route*. This sailing every month combined with the local boat, affords tourists and business men two opportunities of visiting the Hawaiian Islands every four weeks. The Australian Mail boat also calls at Honolulu on its return from the Colonies, so that the facilities for getting back from the Hawaiian Islands equal those for visiting them.

The departure of the Australian Mail steamship is regulated by the arrival at San Francisco of the English Mail for the southern

British Colonies, but the most unvarying punctuality in sailing and arrival is observed with the local boats. The Hawaiian mail is put on board a few minutes before sailing hour—at twelve noon in winter, and two o'clock p. m. in summer, as the season may be, and prompt upon the stroke of the hour, the lines are cast off, the gang-plank is withdrawn, and the noble ship glides into the stream to begin her voyage.

The sailing of the Honolulu steamer is always an event of interest to scores of people, who crowd the ship until the last moment, and afterward line the wharf to catch a parting glimpse of their friends on board. The arrival of each Hawaiian steamer also draws an interested and apparently anxious crowd of people to the Oceanic Company's wharf.

First class excursion tickets to Honolulu and return, good for three months, are issued by the Oceanic Company at reduced rates. Through passengers, to and from Australia, have the option of staying over at Honolulu. Those coming from the Colonies may continue their voyage to San Francisco in one of the local boats without waiting for the next through steamer. This privilege gives an interval of nine days during which the famous volcano of Kilauea, on the island of Hawaii, may be visited, together with all points of interest in and adjacent to Honolulu. In like manner, a through passenger to the Australasian Colonies may take one of the local boats from San Francisco, and having spent twelve most enjoyable days on the Islands, can embark on the Australian Mail boat at Honolulu, and resume his voyage to the antipodes.

The tourist, who for health or pleasure, comes so far West as San Francisco, and omits a visit to the Hawaiian Islands, denies himself a rare enjoyment. He has crossed the American Continent by rail, and subjected himself to the inevitable weariness of an

## INTRODUCTORY.

overland trip. True, he is repaid by the wonders of the West, but if he turn his back on the wonders of the Tropics, so near and so accessible, he is not a thorough traveler. Granting him the wisdom of an experienced sight-seer, he secures passage to Honolulu, and continues his journey by the Oceanic Company's line to "The Paradise of the Pacific." Once on board he is installed in a roomy cabin, fitted with electric light and bell, and furnished with all the conveniences of a room in a first-class hotel. In an hour from the start, the noble ship has passed through the Golden Gate, and the voyager is on the blue Pacific, speeding towards Honolulu.

The voyage is pleasure sailing from beginning to end, day after day bringing fresh delights. Arrived at Honolulu, there lies before the tourist a most interesting and delightful study. He is astonished at the grandeur and luxuriance of the vegetation. The marvelous and ever-changing color of the opaline sea fills him with pleasure and wonder; the soft and fragrant air, the refreshing showers which keep the landscape perpetually green, and the abundant streams of limpid water, thrill him with the realization that he is at last in fairy-land.

### FROM PUNCHBOWL.

"Beyond the ocean's rim the sun dips low,
   A scarlet flame climbs up the western sky ;
The mountain peaks are tipped with roseate glow,
   The golden mists droop over Waianae,
   And cool grey shadows in the valleys lie,
Where laughing waters through deep jungles flow,
And swift-winged birds go flitting to and fro.
   The shadows lengthen as the light grows dim,
   Delicious odors fill the passing breeze ;
   In colors filched from the rainbow's rim,
   Below our feet a wilderness of trees,
     Hides the fair city. Sounding faint and far,
     The muffled music on the coral bar,
The loud-voiced chant of ever restless seas.
          —*Charles H. Ewart.*"

There are so many strange and beautiful things to be seen in the Hawaiian Islands, that it is really difficult to tell the tourist where to begin. Honolulu itself is a bower of beauty, and is, moreover, a place of great historic interest. The ascent of Punchbowl, which overlooks the City, has been rendered easy by the public spirit of the Hawaiian Government, which has built a fine carriage drive to the summit, whence a superb view of the City and harbor, Diamond Head, Pearl River, and the Waianae range is obtained.

A very complete system of street railroads renders travel through the principal thoroughfares of the City and suburbs cheap and expeditious, but most visitors will prefer to view the City leisurely, and enjoy the wealth of foliage and bloom on every side as they stroll along the streets protected from the sun by overshadowing branches.

The tourist, on landing, usually makes his way to the Royal Hawaiian Hotel, a large and commodious building, erected by the Hawaiian Government at heavy expense for the special accommodation of visitors to the Islands. It has been leased by the Government, and is managed as a first-class hostelry on the American plan. It stands in the center of extensive grounds, planted with shade and flowering trees, shrubs and flowers. The rooms are spacious and airy, and the hotel is well provided with baths. An artesian well in the grounds furnishes an unfailing supply of pure water.

The main building is of concrete, two stories high, surrounded by wide verandas, where the guests assemble every evening to enjoy the cool breeze after the heat of the day, or perhaps listen to the music of the Royal Hawaiian band, for whose convenience a permanent stand has been erected in the Hotel grounds. There are several cottages on the grounds for the accommodation of

1. Prison
2. Pali Road
3. Cascade in Iao Valley
4. Cocoanut Island
5. Heights of Haleakala
6. Horned Cattle
7. Haleakala

## INTRODUCTORY.

families or guests who prefer privacy. The Hawaiian Band concerts at the hotel are most enjoyable, and attract large audiences who crowd the grounds as well as the verandas and corridors of the main building. From the hotel tower the eye takes in a wide sweep of valley and plain, sea and mountain, the whole presenting a picture unrivaled for its richness, variety, and warmth of coloring.

There are several well-conducted boarding houses in Honolulu, and those who wish to enjoy the perfection of sea bathing can be accommodated at Waikiki, where there is also a first-class seaside hotel.

Mention has been made of the Royal Hawaiian Band. It was established by the Hon. J. O. Dominis, the late Prince Consort, twenty years ago, and consists of forty pieces. This band, composed wholly of Hawaiians, has been brought to the highest degree of musical skill by Mr. H. Berger, who was sent out specially for this duty by the Prussian Government in 1872, at the request of the late King Kalakaua. Weather permitting, weekly concerts are given by this band at Emma Square, in the City, and Thomas Square, in the suburbs. The band also plays at the Palace functions and occasionally at the Hawaiian Hotel.

The chief places of interest in the City of Honolulu are the Palace and Government Buildings. With proper introduction to the Queen's Chamberlain, access may be had to the Palace, a handsome modern residence, standing in extensive pleasure grounds. The Government Buildings are opposite the Royal Palace, fronting on Palace Square and King street. This is a concrete structure, of considerable architectural merit, and contains the various departmental offices, and the Supreme Court and Judicial Chambers. The Legislature of the Kingdom meets in the main hall of the building, where the sessions of the Supreme Court are also held. In the well-kept grounds of the Government buildings, stands a bronze statue of Kamehameha the Great, in feather helmet and robes of State. The likeness to the founder of the Hawaiian monarchy is said to be perfect.

When Kamehameha completed his conquests, he fixed the seat of his Government at Honolulu, where he discovered a channel through the reef into the only available harbor of the group. As this intelligent sovereign was anxious to promote trade with the outside world, he encouraged shipping to visit the Islands, and in the early days, before the harbor had been surveyed, he went out with his double canoe, manned by eighty to one hundred men, and towed visiting ships inside the reef. Thus the first pilot and harbor master at Honolulu was also the greatest chieftain and most remarkable man of the Hawaiian race.

Kawhaiahoa Church, one of the old landmarks of Honolulu, is in this vicinity. It is built of coral, the material and labor being furnished by the natives soon after their chiefs had renounced idolatry, and is an enduring evidence of the influence of the early Christian missionaries. In the Kawhaiahoa church-yard stands the tomb of King Lunalilo, the last of the Kamehamehas, although he did not assume that name.

The Hawaiian Opera House, a commodious building capable of seating seven hundred people, fronts on Palace square, close to the Government buildings.

A short walk from Palace square will bring the visitor to the Queen's Hospital, built in 1860, in honor of Queen Emma, by her Royal Consort the Fourth Kamehameha, who personally solicited subscriptions for this charity. The grounds surrounding the Queen's Hospital are planted with palms, flowering shrubs and shade trees. The Avenue of Palms, leading up to the main entrance, will well repay a visit.

East of the City, close to the foot hills, and not very far from each other, are Lunalilo Home and Oahu College. The former is surrounded by extensive grounds. It was founded by King Lunalilo, as a home for aged and destitute Hawaiians. Oahu College is also well endowed with lands, and has earned a wide reputation as an educational institution. It is of missionary foundation.

On the west side, a considerable distance from the City, are the Kamehameha schools, founded under the will of Mrs. Bernice Pauahi Bishop, heiress of the late Princess Ruth, sister of Kamehameha the Fifth. They are richly endowed, and consist of preparatory and finishing schools. Practical instruction in useful trades is given to Hawaiian boys and girls, in addition to the regular school course. And here it may be said that the public schools of Honolulu are numerous, well equipped for educational work, and are in charge of a most efficient and zealous body of trained teachers. These remarks apply generally to the public schools of the Kingdom.

The Insane Asylum and Oahu Prison are on the west side, and may be visited on obtaining permission from the proper authority.

The fish market, also the fish ponds in the vicinity of Oahu prison deserve mention. In ancient times many of the shallow places around the coast within the reef barrier were utilized as fish preserves, vast coral enclosures being made by the common people for their chiefs or *aliis*. Many of these fish ponds were abandoned when the lands were divided by Kamehameha the Third, and compulsory labor ceased to be available for the *aliis*.

In the City proper are the Public Library and Reading Room, the Young Men's Christian Association building, containing lecture hall, class rooms and library; also, Odd Fellows' Hall, General Post Office, Custom House, Police buildings and court, Seamen's home, fire stations, telephone offices, etc.

The churches are numerous and well sustained. The English Episcopal Church has established a missionary see at Honolulu, and the Catholic Church has established the bishopric of Olba, also for missionary work. Social and benevolent organizations are also numerous and well supported.

Honolulu is lighted by electricity. It has an efficient water service and fire department. No city in the world is so well or so cheaply supplied by telephone companies as Honolulu, and no other community makes such general use of the telephone.

The population is composed of native Hawaiians, Americans and other persons of European descent, Portuguese chiefly from the Atlantic islands, Chinese and Japanese. This mixed community is orderly and industrious as a rule, and serious crimes are infrequent. The law is strictly enforced.

The conservation of public health is entrusted to a Board of Health, which has large powers, and enjoys public confidence. The Hawaiian Legislature appropriates ten per cent of the gross revenue of the Kingdom for medical and sanitary purposes. The Government maintains a large staff of qualified physicians throughout the Islands, whose duty it is to give medical advice and attendance to native Hawaiians free. Medicine is also supplied gratuitously. The various sugar plantations are required to provide adequate medical and surgical attendance for their laborers, irrespective of race.

There are many charming drives in and around Honolulu, but those to the beach at Waikiki (embracing Kapiolani Park), and to the famous *Pali*, or precipice, over which the all-conquering Kamehameha hurled the vanquished hosts of Oahu, are never overlooked by tourists. Each one is perfect in its way. There is a well made road from the City to the *Pali*, six miles distant. It leads up Nuuanu valley by a gradual ascent to the great cleft in the

A Trip to Hawaii.          *Forbes Co., Boston.*

mountain, ending in an abrupt precipice 1200 feet above sea level. For a considerable distance the road is lined with handsome villas, set in the most beautiful of tropical surroundings. Visitors who are fond of botanizing may gratify their tastes to their hearts' content in any of the valleys between Honolulu and Diamond Head, and yet be within easy reach of the Hotel.

An excursion of nine miles by railroad to Pearl Harbor is one of the attractions of a visit to Honolulu. A new marine resort is springing up at Pearl Harbor since the railroad was built. The scenery is pleasing on this trip, and a glimpse at rice fields, banana plantations and cane fields is obtained.

As the Volcano is the objective point with most visitors to the Hawaiian Islands, care is taken by local organizations to provide proper facilities for reaching and exploring that miracle of nature, the volcano of Kilauea. The Volcano House Company has this business in charge, and provides for sea and land transportation by two routes; also, hotel and guides. A new and commodious Hotel has been built at the Volcano, and visitors may benefit by the health-giving properties of its famous sulphur baths. The scenery by either route presents a series of charming and often impressive tropical views.

It is needless to attempt a description of the weird ghastliness of the great crater of Kilauea, or the active lake, Halemaumau,—"House of Everlasting Fire"—which occupies its southern end. This lake changes in appearance so frequently that no single description would fit. It is one of the most sublime and awe-inspiring sights in the world, and must be seen to be understood or appreciated. Nor is it necessary in this place to repeat the legends of Hawaiian mythology about the Goddess Pele, whose throne is supposed to be in the midst of this seething, spouting lake of liquid earth. These will be told by the guides under conditions which heighten their effect, and account for the credulity of the ancient Hawaiians. Visitors to the Volcano usually secure specimens of Pele's hair and other kinds of lava.

There are many places worth visiting on the Hawaiian Islands as well as the Volcano of Kilauea. In some respects a visit to the vast extinct crater of Haleakala—"House of the Sun"—is quite as interesting as a visit to Halemaumau. It presents the evidence of far more stupendous activity than Kilauea ever could show. The crater is 2,000 feet deep, with a circumference of about twenty miles and a diameter of seven and a half miles. Two immense gaps on the east and north side show where the molten lava, in a stream seven miles wide, poured out of this great crater, draining it of its molten contents. Standing above the clouds in the early morning, on the edge of this huge pit, one sees vast masses of clouds rushing into the crater through the clefts already spoken of, filling with fleecy billows its sixteen square miles of space; then the sun appears, and the clouds are expelled as they came, leaving his house or palace flooded with his golden light.

There are ruins of heathen temples on Maui accessible to tourists, but they would probably be more interested in the evidences of industrial enterprise which abound on that island, in common with other islands of the group. The most productive cane fields in the world are on Maui; as also the largest sugar plantation. Spreckelsville plantation contains 40,000 acres, of which 12,000 acres are always in cultivation. This plantation is cultivated by irrigation, and the cost of bringing the water on the land and the engineering difficulties overcome were very great. The mill is capable of manufacturing 120 tons of sugar per day. Steam-ploughs are employed in cultivation, and a standard guage steel railroad traverses the cane fields for miles, carrying cane and passengers.

## INTRODUCTORY.

Maui has been aptly styled the Switzerland of the Hawaiian group. A visit to it, however, is not included in the Volcano trip, but it may be easily accomplished if time admits. Similarly a visit to Kauai, the "Garden Isle," and its famous "barking sands," and picturesque scenery must be undertaken separately.

# A TRIP TO HAWAII.

A GREAT deal has been written and published about this most picturesque and delightful land, but the most poetic, as it is by far the most enjoyable sketch of all, is from the pen of Charles Warren Stoddard, a well known litterateur and former resident of the Hawaiian Islands, published in 1885, by the Passenger Department of the Oceanic Steamship Company. His description of the sea voyage to Honolulu, what the tourists saw there, and how they spent their time on the Islands is as fresh and appropriate to-day as it was when it came from his facile pen. The following extracts from this charming brochure are reprinted for the special enjoyment of visitors to the Paradise of the Pacific. An accurate map is found in this little book which will give the tourist the geographical position of the Kingdom of Hawaii, and of the various islands in the group.

## "HOW IT HAPPENED."*

We are seven semi-invalids, frost-bitten or sun-struck, world weary, full of disgust and malaria, and we resolve to join hands and set forth in search of life and liberty in a new land.

---

* *A Trip to Hawaii* by CHARLES WARREN STODDARD, 1885.

# OCEANIC STEAMSHIP CO.

### FLEET:

| ALAMEDA. | 3000 Tons | MARIPOSA. | 3000 Tons |
| AUSTRALIA. | | ZEALANDIA. | |

OCEANIC STEAMSHIP CO.'S S. S. MARIPOSA.—3000 Tons.

Hawaii, the celebrated Sandwich Islands, being the nearest available corner of the Antipodes, we take round tickets for the Hawaiian tour, and instantly prepare to emigrate.

Hawaii, the most written about, and the least understood little kingdom in the world; the prettiest, wildest, weirdest, most unique conglomeration of Paradise and Perdition on record, within easy sail of San Francisco, and having semi-monthly steamers plying to and fro with the regularity of a weaver's shuttle; Hawaii lures us with its legend, landscape and poetry, and we embark without delay.

\* \* \*

## II.

Extracts from the Log of the "Mariposa":

"O, had we some bright little Isle of our own,
In the blue summer Ocean, far off and alone."

Seven of us stood in bright array; brides, benedicts and bachelors; waving a fond farewell from the upper deck. We were not alone, for the cabins were full, but we were not making acquaintances at that moment, and so we stood in silhouette waving our fond farewell—in fact, seven of them, from the deck of the "Mariposa."

At 3 p. m. sharp, the gang-plank was hauled ashore, and we swung off into the stream. Never before in history did a ship leave port so promptly, but as we are warranted to arrive on time, we can easily pardon this very business-like beginning of a pleasure trip to Hawaii.

In exactly seven days from the date of our departure, we are to enter the harbor of Honolulu, and at the witching hour of noon.

Meanwhile, music and mirth reign in the Social Hall; cigarettes and droll stories in the smoking room, while symptoms of frolics and flirtations pervade the ship from stem to stern. The mists gathered with the first evening shades, but we were well away from the Coast by this time, and we felt that the voyage was prosperously begun.

For a couple of days we were reminded of the land we had left. An eager and a nipping air blew over us, the troubled sea was a measureless waste of cold suds and bluing. Sometimes a solitary sail flickered for an hour on the horizon, and was the subject of much conjecture, but most of the day was passed between the piano, the library, the smoking room and the constitutional spurts which converted the long deck of the "Mariposa" into an arena for the physical development of the go-as-you-please passengers.

Then came a gradual transition: sky and sea grew brighter and more exquisitely blue; we were hastening towards the calms of Cancer. The temperate atmosphere—it is too often intemperate in the temperate zone—was already becoming semi-tropical. The great ports of the ship stood wide open to the balmy breeze. The decks were filled with loungers. From the Social Hall at twilight, floated the half melancholy refrain of a waltz. Light feet skimmed the deck, and between the floods of moonlight and the silver sea, the joyous coteries in the saloon—where a wilderness of electric lights glowed like loops of red-gold, and made summer sunshine, bright as day—the minstrelsy and the delicious languor that was beginning to possess us, the "Mariposa" was like a floating *Casino* drifting toward Paradise on an even keel.

In the tropics at last! Such a flat, oily sea it was then; so transparent that we saw great fish swimming about 'full fathom five' beneath us. A monstrous shark swam lazily past, his dorsal fin glistening like polished steel, and now and again cutting the surface of the sea like a knife, his brace of pilot fish darting hither and thither like little one-legged harlequins.

Flat-headed gonies sat high on the water, piping their querulous note as they tugged at something edible, a dozen of them entering into the domestic difficulty. One after another would desert the cause, run a little way over the sea to get a good start, leap heavily into the air, sail about for a few minutes, and then drop back upon the sea feet foremost and skate for a yard or two, making a white mark and a pleasant sound as they slid over the water.

The exquisite Nautilus floated past us with its gauzy sail set, looking like a thin slice cut out of a soap bubble; the weird Anemone laid its pale, sensitive petals on the tips of the waves, and panted in ecstacy. Down dropt the swarthy sun into his tent of cloud; the waves were of amber; the fervid sky was flushed; it seemed as if something splendid were about to happen up there in the heavens, and that the secret could be kept no longer. The purplest twilight followed, wherein the sky blossomed all over with the biggest, ripest, goldenest stars; such stars as hang like fruits in sun-fed orchards; such stars as lay a track of fire in the sea; such stars as rise and set over misty mountain tops and beyond low green capes, like young moons, every one of them.

The past was forgotten; Hawaii seemed the one thing needful, and we clicked glasses that night and fell upon one another's necks in mutual congratulation, for it was our last night on board, and already we were conjuring spells of barbarous enchantment of snow-white reefs baptized with silver spray, girdling the Islands of the Blessed. Already we seemed to see the broad fan-leaves of the banana droop in the motionless air, and through the tropical night the palms aspired to heaven as we lay dreaming our sea dreams in the cradle of the deep.

## III.

> "Hawaii nei—of many one thou art,
> Each scattered fragment an essential part.
> No jeweled setting is more fair than thee,
> O em'rald cluster in a beryl sea!
> Thy life is music—Fate, the notes prolong!
> Each isle a stanza and the whole a song."
>
> —*Geo. H. Stewart.*

On the morning of the seventh day, an island rises like a small blue cloud out of the sea; then another, and yet another, and toward the last, we make our way. Green with a verdure that never fades; brown with the bronze tints of lava-flows that have been cold for centuries; a beach of dazzling whiteness, fringed with groves of cocoa palms; the sea like a huge emerald, with sunshine reflected upon the coral bottom, and brilliantly tinted fish sporting about us;—it is thus that we approach Honolulu at noon on the seventh day.

Looking at Diamond Head from the sea, the volcanic shore promises nothing of the beauty that is harbored in the vernal vales beyond it; but the moment our good ship rounds the point of the famous head-land, the fairy-like coast line is suddenly revealed.

It is a transformation scene. The mountains turn gloriously green. Valleys, vistas in Eden, dawn upon the eye in quick succession. The sea rises in long voluptuous waves and fawns upon the reef, while within the surf the tranquil water is like a tideless river, where only the water-lilies are lacking; but in their stead, are troops of Hawaiian swimmers—veritable water nymphs—with a profusion of glossy locks floating about their shoulders like seaweed. Of course we are all impatience, for in less than an hour we shall come to shore in the Kingdom where a century ago, (1778),

HANAPEPA FALLS.

1. Hawaiian boy with the piece of coin
2. Line of Oahu Railway
3. Native Divers waiting for the coin
4. Road to Volcano of Kilauea
5. Road out of Honolulu
6. Banana Plant

Captain Cook, the great navigator, met his fate—"As he sailed, as he sailed."

There is hardly time to note well the picturesque features of the landscape and marine, the white sands at Waikiki, the feathery forest of algeroba trees that now overshadow the plains, the russet slopes of Old Punch Bowl—a domesticated crater just back of the town—and the roofs of the Capital, inundated with verdure; a summer city, such as the birds might build between the mountains and the sea. Then we turn abruptly towards the land, thread a narrow channel between submerged walls of coral, and are soon within speaking distance of friends who have come to the shore to give us welcome.

By this time the sea is littered with cocoanuts, but they are curly headed, most of them, and clamorous, for the dime-divers of Hawaii doff their garments at the shortest notice and disport themselves amphibiously so long as there is a prospect of raising another nickel out of the vasty deep.

Canoes dart upon the water as if they were living things, part fish, part flesh, part fowl, with one skeleton wing for an outrigger, a fin paddle, and a bare, brown Kanaka amidships. Fish baptize themselves by immersion in space, and keep leaping into the air like momentary inches of chain lightning; there is the perpetual boom of the surf, the clang of joy-bells on shore, and a possible shower in the refreshing cloud that is stealing down from the heights. "Three cheers and a tiger,"—for the voyage has come to an end.

The gang-plank is out again. There is a wild embrace all around, a brief interview with the officers of the Customs, and we divide ourselves among the numerous carriages awaiting patronage on the dock, and are at once driven to the Hawaiian Hotel, at the rate of two for a quarter of a dollar.

Here are semi-detached villas, cosy cottages for the brides and benedicts, and chambers with venetian blinds and broad verandas, vine shaded and musical birds, for the repose of the bachelors; but of course we fly at once to the cupola of the establishment to take our reckoning. It is a little glass-house above the tree tops, and out of reach. We look down upon palace and hovel, and find that the hovel is perhaps the better ventilated of the two, and that there is no end of love with the dinner of herbs therein. Indeed, the Kingdom seems to us like an island of tranquil delights, with *Repose* written in large letters all over it. Here we have no hateful game more majestic than the mosquito; here the noblest victim of the chase is the agile flea; now and again, though rarely, appears that chain of unpleasant circumstances, the centipede, or perchance, the devil-tailed scorpion, whose stroke is by no means fatal, reminds us that nothing can touch us further; and, indeed, but for these foreign invaders—they all came in with civilization—this life were almost too Edenesque.

The marvelous temperature, which is never hot and never cold —70 to 90 degrees Fah. all the year round, with a few extra showers to emphasize the winter months; the rich and variable color; the fragrance so intense after a shower, when the ginger and the Japanese lily seem to distil perfume, drop by drop; the tinkle of gay guitars; the spray-like notes dashed from shuddering lute-strings; the irreproachable languor of a race that is the incarnation of all these elements—this is quite as much as man wants here below (Lat. 21° 18′ 23″, Lon. 157° 4′ 45″), and all this he has without the asking.

What if the impertinent Mynah perch upon the roof and fill the attic with strange noises? What if they infest the groves at twilight, and deluge the land with cascades of silvery sound? They are a pert bird that has rid the Kingdom of its caterpillars, and now they propose to luxuriate for the rest of their natural lives.

It was the war-whoop of a Mynah bird on the window-sill that called our attention to old Diamond Head, which at that moment was glowing like a live coal, the picture of a red-hot volcano with the smoke rubbed out; there was a strip of beryl sea behind it, and at its base a great plain fretted with the light green shade of the Algeroba—this was framed in the sashes on one side of the cupola.

On another side, mountain peaks buried their brows in cloud and wept copiously, so sentimental was the hour of our communion; forests of the juiciest green drank these showers of tears.

Turning again, we saw the sun-burnt hills beyond Palama, and the crisp cones of the small volcanoes, and more sea, and then the exquisite outline of the Waianae mountains, of a warm, dusty purple, and with a film of diffused rainbows floating in the middle distance.

Has not the poet sung of Waianae:

> "No sound is on the shore
> Save reef-bound breakers roar,
> Or distant boatman's song, or sea birds cry;
> And hushed the inland bay,
> In stillness far away,
> Like phantoms rise the hills of Waianae."

There was but one window left; it opened upon a sea stretching to the horizon, and mingling with the sky, a shore fringed with tapering masts, and crested, sentinel palms; and beneath us the city submerged in billowy foliage through which the wind stirred in gusts and eddies.

We wondered where we were and in what season, and then, after a diligent study of globes and calendars, we laughed to scorn the amateur geographers who vainly confound us with Tahiti, or sweep us away toward New Guinea or the uttermost parts.

The fact is, following our air line due east from the hotel cupola, we trip on the tail of Lower California, plunge through the heart of Mexico into the Caribbean Sea, dash across Cuba, and are lost in the Atlantic; westward, we plough the solitary sea crossing the track of Laputa, the "Flying Island," just escape Luggnagg, and more is the pity, for "the Luggnaggers are a polite and generous people," says Gulliver; we see Hongkong, Calcutta, Mecca. and, beyond the Red sea, the Nile waters and the measureless sands of the Sahara.

And then we hold our breath for a moment when we think how far above us and below us rolls the everlasting deep from pole to pole.

The evening and the morning were the first day, and the first experience was ended—an experience bound in green and gold, the green of the grassy hills, and the gold of the sun-lit sea. We had monopolized the cupola to the despair of those guests who fly to it as to a haven of rest; but there was no further thought of monopoly in our minds, for the afterglow was overwhelming, and already from the cool corridors of the caravansary—a caravansary that in its architecture reminds one of Singapore—sweetly and silently ascended the incense of the evening meal.

IV.

The cocoa, with its crest of spears,
    Stands sentry 'round the crescent shore,
The algeroba bent with years,
    Keeps watch beside the lanai door.
The cool winds fan the mango's cheek,
    The mynah flits from tree to tree,
And zephyrs to the roses speak
    Their sweetest words at Waikiki.

> Like truant children of the deep
>   Escaped behind a coral wall,
> The lisping wavelets laugh and leap,
>   Nor heed old ocean's stern recall.
> All day they frolic with the sands,
>   Kiss pink-lipped shells in wanton glee,
> Make windrows with their patting hands,
>   And singing, sleep at Waikiki.
>
> O Waikiki! O scene of peace!
>   O home of beauty and of dreams!
> No haven in the Isles of Greece
>   Can chord the harp to sweeter themes;
> For houris haunt the broad lanais,
>   While scented zephyrs cool the lea,
> And, looking down from sunset skies,
>   The angels smile on Waikiki.
>
> —*Rollin M. Daggett.*

We take our turns in the hammock devising plans for the day; there is nothing so easy in life as to swing, thus measuring off the hours in luxurious and rhythmical vibrations. The hammock has its vicissitudes; sometimes it is a pale invalid who retires into it as into a chrysalis, and is rocked to and fro in the wind; then the sympathetic and sociable gather about it, and subject the patient to the smoke cure—of course "by special command"—or the mint-julep cure, or to bits of frivolous converse thrown in between a matinee-reception-concert at the Princess Regent's, or a band-night at Emma Square. Sometimes a bewildered guest from the Colonies, or elsewhere, rolls into it and sleeps with all his might and main; sometimes a whole row of children trail their slim legs over the side of it, which is all that saves them from being compared to peas in a pod.

The breeze blows fresh from the mountains, the health-giving trade wind; we can look right up the green glade which is the gateway to Mount Tantalus and see the clouds torn to shreds across the wooded highlands; we can watch the mango trees where the mangoes hang like bronze plummets, and the monkey-pods in bloom, their tops resembling terraced gardens; now and again, the *Kamani* sheds a huge leaf as big as a beefsteak, and as red as a raw one; but what are these splashes of color to the *Ponciana Regia!* It is a conflagration!

The *Bugainvillæa*, a cataract of magenta blossoms that look like artificial leaves just out of a chemical bath, obtrudes itself at intervals; it is the only crude bit of color in a landscape where the majority of the trees are colossal boquets at one season or another.

The Hibiscus is aglow with flowers of flame the whole year round, and the land is overrun with brilliant creepers even to the eaves of the hotel, where the birds quarrel and call noisily from dawn to dusk.

Thus we lounge in a land where all mankind lounges a portion of the day; where it is not considered indelicate for a merchant to pose in the midst of his merchandise guiltless of coat or vest, for his respectability is established beyond question, and his bank account a patent fact; where ladies drive in morning *en deshabille*, and shop on the curb-stone without alighting from their carriages, and where any of them may pay an evening call unbonneted and unattended.

But what should we do to be saved from shameless indolence? First ride or drive to the beach and bathe in a sea that rolls up warm from the Equator. We can go *en masse* in the 'bus,* or we can foot it if we are touched with the pedestrian craze, for three miles even in this climate are not too many for an appetizer.

One may plunge for hours in the reef-girdled lagoon at Waikiki

---

* The primitive 'bus is now supplanted by a street railroad.

without fear of taking a chill; there are bathing suits there, and canoes, and a long easy swell on which to undulate; and there is the Park to ride or drive in, and the beautiful highways and the more beautiful byways between the Park and the Town, where every sense is gratified at the self-same moment. It is a delicious life we lead at Waikiki; those that dwell there habitually know the range of its possibilities; they drift townward at a convenient hour pleading business engagements. The town, the business portion of it, runs like a mechanical piano, and if you will only give it time, some one or another will wind it up, and then it will play its pretty chorus of summer toil as gaily as if it were so many bars out of a light Opera; a jingle of musical coin that is kept up till 5 p. m., when all at once it shuts up or runs down, and life at the beach really begins.

It begins with a sunset across a tropic sea, and a twilight that seems longer than common in this vicinity; sometimes there are shadowy ships in this twilight, and there are always canoes enough afloat to make one wish to quote the easy lines about "autumnal leaves" and "brooks in Valombrosa."

Then comes dinner, and then moonlight and music on sea and shore, and naked fishermen bearing aloft huge torches that gild their bronze brown bodies; and bathers under the stars, and torchlight fishing with trusty retainers beyond the silvery surf.

So end the evenings and the mornings of days that are much alike; but not for worlds would we vary them, especially such nights as these, when the moon is an opal and the stars emeralds, and the whole wonderful picture of Earth, Sea and Sky is done in seventeen shades of green !

## V.

"We have had enough of action, and of motion ; we
Roll'd to starboard, roll'd to larboard, when the surge was seething free,
Where the wallowing monster spouted his foam-fountains in the sea.

Let us swear an oath, and keep it with an equal mind
In the hollow Lotus-land to live and lie reclined,
On the hills like Gods together, careless of mankind."
— *Tennyson.*

Every new arrival in Honolulu goes to the *Pali*, at the top of Nuuanu Valley, as soon as the excursion can be arranged; even the through passengers by the Australian boats, who are but six hours in port, secure carriages or horses, and at once set forth rejoicing, for the prospect from the *Pali*—the precipice—is superb, and the round trip can be made for a few dollars, and leisurely enough in three or four hours.

There are carriages for the accommodation of three people; wagonettes that seat a half dozen, and a big coach and four for larger parties, and these may be telephoned for at a moment's notice from the office of the Hotel.

Some of us went on wheels and some in saddles. Corkscrews and sandwiches were not forgotten; nor field-glasses, the most indispensable of all.

The way lies through shady avenues, between residences that stand in the midst of broad lawns and among foliage of the most brilliant description. An infinite variety of palms and tropical plants, with leaves of enormous circumference, diversify the landscape.

A Trip to Hawaii.

Forbes Co., Boston.

## NUUANU AVENUE.

We pass the long line of villas on Nuuanu Avenue; cross the bridge where sudden freshets sometimes sweep like tidal waves from the mountains to the sea; pass trim gardens that resemble Japanese landscapes, by native artists, and neglected gardens that are like jungles of cacti and bamboo; pass the gray walled cemeteries with their clusters of funereal cypresses, and the Royal Mausoleum where the tall *Kahilis*—those emblems of savage royalty—still stand with bedraggled feathers in memory of the late Princess Keelikolani, the last of the Kamehamehas;* pass the Chinese tea-houses by the way side, and the kalo patches and plantations of bananas and the summer palace of Dowager Queen Emma with its stately white columns shining in the grove, and finally the grimy walls of a forgotten palace of an almost forgotten King.

Thus having quit the town we slowly ascend the cool, green valley where the rapid streams gurgle in the long grass by the road-side, and the valley walls grow high and steep and close; where the convolvulus tumbles a cataract of blossoms at our feet and creepers go mad and swamp a whole forest under billows of green; where there are leafy hammocks to swing in, and leafy towers to climb in, and leafy dungeons to bury one's self out of sight in. We drink copious draughts of delicious mountain water;

---

* The "emblems of savage royalty" spoken of above long since gave place to others in honor of the late Queen Emma, widow of Kamehameha the Fourth; and these in turn were replaced by Kahilis in honor of Princess Likelike, mother of the present Heir Apparent, Princess Kaiulani (whose likeness appears in our illustrated title-page), and sister of the late King Kalakaua, in whose honor the "tall Kahilis" now stand at the Royal Mausoleum in the beautiful and romantic Nuuanu Cemetery.

we rejoice mightily ; even a shower of shining rain doesn't dampen our ardor—no one seems to heed it here.

Under the shadow of a great rock we camp, and then climb the little rise to the brow of the precipice, and look over into the other world. For a long time we are silent. I don't believe people ever talk much here; in the first place, if you open your mouth too wide you can't shut it again without getting under the lee of something—the wind blows so hard. But who wants to talk when he is perched on the back-bone of an island with fifteen hundred feet of space beneath him, and the birds swimming about in it liked winged fish in a transparent sea?

And Oh, the silent land beyond the heights, with the long, long, winding, rocky stairway leading down into it ! No sound ever comes from that beautiful land, not even from the marvelously blue sea that noiselessly piles its breakers upon the shore like swan's-down.

A great mountain wall divides this side of Oahu into about equal parts; it is half in sunshine and half in shade. On the one hand is the metropolis, on the other semi-solitude and peace. Peace! a visible, tangible peace, with winding roads in it, and patches of bright sugar cane, and wee villages and palm trees upon the distant shore; it is picturesque in form and delicious in color; something to look at in awe and wonderment and to turn from at last with a doubt of its reality.

Microscopic pilgrims toil up the long stairway—fugitives from the mysterious land down yonder; we are almost surprised to find that they are human, like ourselves. While some come back to us from the tour of this newly discovered country, others are going thither—passing down into the silence and the serenity of the enchanting distance, and becoming as ghosts in dream-land. The havenward vista is glorious. The harbor as seen from the *Pali* reminds one of the Vesuvian bay, and the golden-crested combers play like sheet lightning upon the surf. What a pilgrimage it is and who that has made it will ever forget it?


## VI.

> "Muse of the many twinkling feet, whose charms
> Are now extended up from legs to arms;
> Terpsichore !—too long misdeemed a maid—
> Reproachful term—bestowed but to upbraid—
> Henceforth in all the bronze of brightness shine,
> The least a vestal of the Virgin Nine,"
> —*Byron.*

The most characteristic feature of Hawaiian life, commonly known as a relic of barbarism, is still to be seen in the capital of the Kingdom, though it is usually under cover.

It is the Hula-Hula, the national dance, and it may be obtained in quantities to suit within a stone's throw of the Hotel; it is the spontaneous production of the populous and prolific soil that lies round about that extraordinary settlement known in Honolulu as the Mosquito Fleet.

The origin of the name which will long be associated with a very central, yet very secret quarter of Honolulu is this: In the beginning was the Kalo-patch—Kalo is pronounced as if it were spelled *taro;* nothing can be prettier than a well kept Kalo-patch; a lake full of deflowered calla-lilies might resemble it; when seen from a little distance, and especially from a height, a disk of burnished silver, across which green enameled arrow-headed leaves in high relief are set in lozenge pattern, could not be more attractive; but the trail of the mosquito is over them all.

There was a time when the narrow paths that ran between the Kalo-patches in the quarter of which I write, led from one grass house to another; grass houses, like mushrooms, cropped up almost anywhere, but especially beside still waters, and so it came to pass that a little village, a toy Venice, sat watching its reflection in the unruffled like waters of the Kalo-patches and the voice of the multitudinous mosquito in the vicinity was like a chorus of buzz saws; the place was known to Jack-a-shore as the Mosquito Fleet, and therein his feet went astray with alacrity.

The Kalo was long since pulled and beaten and eaten in fistsfull of succulent poi; the patches have been filled in and sodded over, and the grass houses have given place to miserable wooden shanties, but the original crookedness of the lane that led to destruction is preserved.

We made our accidental entrance on one occasion, and traversed what seemed to be a *cul-de-sac;* at the last moment we were shifted as if by magic into a passage hardly broader than our shoulders, and but twenty paces long; all at once a diminutive village sprung up about us; we felt like discoverers and wandered jubilantly about among houses with strips of gardens nestling between them, and all of these fitted together like the bits of a Chinese puzzle. Now it was quite impossible to be certain of anything, for the lane, which seemed without beginning and without end, turned unexpected corners with bewildering frequency, and, though we succeeded in threading the perilous mazes, the wonder was that we didn't stumble into windows that unexpectedly opened upon us, and through doors that aptly blocked the way. We met no one in that narrow path; had we done so, one or the other must needs have backed out, or vaulted the fence beyond which it were not seemly to penetrate.

There was music, as there always is music where two or three natives are gathered together; a chant, half nasal, half guttural, such as the mud wasp makes in his cell, relieved by the boom of the agitated calabash, and the clang of the heavy feet upon the floor.

It was the Hula-Kui, the dance of the athletes, immensely popular to-day, but in reality the revival of a very ancient dance, in which the participants rival one another in vigorous posturing and graceful and expressive gesticulation.

\*    \*    \*    \*

The veritable Hula-Hula was to follow. There was a murmur of admiration as a band of beautiful girls, covered with wreaths of flowers and vines, entered and seated themselves before us. While the musicians beat an introductory overture on the tom-toms, the dancers proceeded to bind shawls or scarfs about their waists turban-fashion. They sat in a line facing us, elbow to elbow. Their upper garments were of the airiest description; their bosoms were scarcely hidden by the necklace of jasmine that rested upon them.

Then the master of the ceremonies, who sat, gray-headed and wrinkled, at one end of the room, threw back his head and uttered a long, wild and shrill guttural—a kind of invocation to the goddess of the dance. When this clarion cry had ended, the dance began, all joining in it with wonderful rhythm, the body swaying slowly backward and forward, to left and right; the arms tossing, or rather waving in the air above the head; now beckoning some spirit of light, so tender and seductive were the emotions of the dancers, so graceful and free the movements of the wrists; and anon, with violence and fear they seemed to repulse a host of devils that hovered invisibly about them.

The spectators watched and listened breathlessly, fascinated by the terrible wildness of the song, and the monotonous thrumming of the accompaniment. Presently the excitement increased; swifter and more wildly the bare arms beat the air, embracing as it were, the airy forms that haunted the dancers who now rose to their knees and with astonishing agility, caused the clumsy draperies about their loins to quiver with an undulatory motion, increasing or decreasing in violence, according to the sentiment of the song and the enthusiasm of the spectators.

The room whirled with the reeling dancers, who seemed each encircled with a living serpent in the act of swallowing big lumps of something from his throat clean to the tip of his tail, and these convulsions continued till the hysterical dancers staggered and fell to the floor, overcome by unutterable fatigue.

Meanwhile, windows and doors were packed full of strange, wild faces, and the frequent police gently soothed the clamoring populace without, who, having eyes saw not—which is probably the acme of aggravation.

## VII.

> "O hundred shores of happy clime,
> How swiftly steam'd ye by the bark!
> At times the whole sea burned, at times
> With wakes of fire we tore the dark;
> At times a carven craft would shoot
> From havens hid in fairy bowers,
> With naked limbs and flowers and fruit,
> But we nor paused for fruit nor flowers."
> —*Tennyson.*

Every Tuesday, at 5 p. m., a steamer leaves Honolulu for the windward islands of the group, chief of which is Hawaii, with its fountain of everlasting fire.

The once famous craft, the *Like Like*, has given place to a more commodious steamer, the *Kinau*. On the *Like Like*, passengers who preferred balmy sea-breezes to the air of the cabin, were wont to camp out on deck, where the mirth and minstrelsy of the Hawaiians made night a novelty. The *Kinau* has staterooms for the accommodation of those who love privacy, and moreover, being a fast boat, she has shortened the short trip to Hawaii by some hours; it can be made easily in four and twenty.

In the twilight, after leaving Honolulu, we are in the middle sea between two islands that float like rosy clouds on the horizon.

About 9 p. m., we pass Molokai, the mysterious land whither are banished the unfortunate lepers. Then there is another channel, and beyond it three islands, Maui, Lanai and Kahoolaui; at the former we touch, before midnight, dropping anchor off Lahaina. Lahaina is a little slice of civilization beached on the shore of barbarism; a charming, drowsy and dreamy village with one broad street; a street with but one side to it, for the sea laps over the sloping sands on its lower edge, and the sun sets right in the face of the citizens just as they are going to supper.

It is true that there are two or three long and narrow lanes overhung with a green roof of leaves, and there are summer houses with hammocks pitched close upon the white edge of the shore—but all this we see as through a glass, darkly, for the *Kinau* tarries but an hour in the roadstead and the moonlight, when we trip anchor and hasten on our voyage.

This souvenir of one of the prettiest and most tropical corners in the Kingdom, once the capital of the Kingdom and the favorite of the Kamehamehas, we bring away with us :

### LAHAINA.

Where the wave tumbles ;
Where the reef rumbles ;
Where the sea sweeps
  Under bending palm branches,
Sliding its snow-white
  And swift avalanches :
Where the sails pass
O'er an ocean of glass,
  Or trail their dull anchors
Down in the sea-grass.

Where the hills smoulder ;
Where the plains smoke ;
Where the peaks shoulder
  The clouds like a yoke ;
Where the dear isle
Has a charm to beguile,
  As she lies in the lap
Of the seas that enfold her.
Where shadows falter ;
Where the mist hovers
Like steam that covers
Some ancient altar.

Where the sky rests
On deep wooded crests ;
  Where the clouds lag :
Where the sun floats
His glittering moats,
Swimming the rainbows
  That girdle the crag.

Where the new comer
In deathless summer
  Dreams away troubles ;
Where the grape blossoms
  And blows its sweet bubbles ;

A Trip to Hawaii.

Forbes Co., Boston.

Where the goats cry
  From the hill side corral ;
Where the fish leaps
  In the weedy canal—
In the shallow lagoon
  With its waters forsaken ;
Where the dawn struggles
  With night for an hour,
Then breaks like a tropical
  Bird from its bower.

Where from the long leaves
  The fresh dew is shaken ;
Where the wind sleeps
  And where the birds waken !

An hour later we pause at Maalaea, and feel the spray and the sand blown from off the windy isthmus of Maui. At dawn, we reach Makena, the port of that paradise in mid-air, Ulupalakua,— "Ripe bread-fruit for the gods"—two-thousand feet above us ; then another channel, the last, is crossed, and early in the day we hug the shores of Hawaii, running in and out, dropping passengers and freight and live stock—the latter are dropped into the sea— and so we are afforded an agreeable variety in a voyage which is too brief to be monotonous. The weather-side of the giant island is a series of magnificent precipices, that in many cases overhang the sea, and until we reach Hilo, our port of destination, we cannot withdraw from the splendid coastline our fascinated gaze.

Rich and radiant valleys are folded in between those verdant heights. Between Hilo and the valley of Waipio. a distance of less than sixty miles, there are ninety-two ravines, each with its torrent rushing downward to the sea, many of them with waterfalls, and one of these waterfalls, in the Waipio valley, makes a sheer leap of 1,700 feet from the clouds into a forest of bread-fruit trees.

Most of the seaward precipices are from 1,000 to 1,500 feet in height, and from all of these, after every shower, descend innumerable streams; it is a veritable realization of the Lotus-eaters' dream:

> "In the afternoon they came unto a land,
> In which it seemed always afternoon.
> All round the coast the languid air did swoon,
> Breathing like one that hath a weary dream.
> Full faced above the valley stood the moon,
> And like a downward smoke, the slender stream
> Along the cliff to fall, and pause, and fall did seem.
>
> A land of streams! Some like a downward smoke,
> Slow-dropping veils of thinnest lawn, did go;
> And some through wavering lights and shadows broke,
> Rolling a slumberous sheet of foam below.
> They saw the gleaming river seaward flow
> From the inner land; far off, three mountain tops,
> Three silent pinnacles of aged snow,
> Stood sunset flushed; and dewed with showery drops,
> Up clomb the shadowy palm above the woven copse."
>
> —*Tennyson.*

## VIII.

> "See how the tall palms lift their locks
> From mountain clefts—what vales,
> Basking beneath the noontide sun,
> That high and hotly sails!
>
> Yet all about the breezy shore,
> Unheedful of the glow,
> Look how the children of the South
> Are passing to and fro!
>
> What noble forms! What fairy place!
> Cast anchor in this cove,
> Push out the boat, for in this land
> A little we must rove!"
>
> —*William Howitt.*

Hilo is a cluster of summer houses hidden among palms and bread-fruit trees, where the rain is said to fall perpetually; perhaps it is for this reason that Hilo is the most tropical in appearance, as it is certainly the most beautiful of Hawaiian hamlets.

What a shore it has! A crescent with a row of houses facing it, where the tenants seem to have little else to do than

> "To watch the crisping ripples on the beach,
> The tender curving lines of creamy spray."

We find other occupation, for there are delightful drives in the vicinity; to Cocoa-nut Island, to the Rainbow Waterfalls, to the neighboring heights where the best view of the coast is obtained—and a marvelous view it is; and also to the last lava-flow, a spectacle of surpassing interest.

No where else in the world are there such lava fields, so easily approached, so varied, so extensive. In 1880, a volcanic wound was opened in the flank of Mauna Loa, and for nine months a river of red-hot lava flowed steadily toward the sea. Most of the time one might have walked in front of it, its progress was so slow. About the camps of visitors the air quivered with the heat of the all-devouring flood, and the glare of burning forests through which it ploughed, made night perpetual day.

At that time, Hilo was in imminent danger, and the inhabitants were preparing for flight, when the flow ceased almost upon the edge of the town. The more superstitious natives believe that Hilo was spared through the intercession or by the command of the late Princess Keelikolani, who, with her people, made a pilgrimage to the lava stream, and, having paid a tribute of propitiatory offerings to *Pele*, the Goddess of the Volcano, the stream was suddenly stayed after having flowed a distance of nearly fifty miles; a single house was destroyed and no lives were lost, but the iron waves of that fearful flood remain to mark its course forever.

Hilo is a place of rest; there are excellent accommodations for those who wish to tarry in a spot where the inhabitants lead a kind of dream-life, and where the chief event of the week is the arrival of the steamer from Honolulu with a budget of news from the outer world.

A Trip to Hawaii.

Forbes Co.— Boston.

# HOW IT HAPPENED.

## IX.

> "We'll wander on through wood and field,
> We'll sit beneath the vine;
> We'll drink the limpid cocoa-milk,
> And pluck the native pine.
>
> The bread-fruit and cassava-root,
> And many a glowing berry,
> Shall be our feast; for here, at least,
> Why should we not be merry!"
>
> Wm. Howitt.

It is a fact, that the thirty mile horse-back ride from Hilo to the crater of Kilauea is not as comfortable as it might be under other circumstances; that the trail is not the best in the world, nor the horses either; and that it rains at intervals on the road; but water-proofs are obtainable, one may lodge at a half-way house, and thus break the journey into two easy stages, and, as for the object of the pilgrimage, does it not well repay one for some little privation and fatigue?*

We stop over at the Half-way House for the sake of an experience; it is not on every day that one finds an excuse for looking into the inner life of the gentle Hawaiian, so we order supper, and secretly take notes during the preparation thereof.

In turning over my journals, I find the record of a night spent under a grass roof, and I give it as the faithful picture of an episode I would not willingly forget.

---

* This was in 1885; there is now a well made carriage road the greater part of the way, between Hilo and Volcano House at Kilauea. There is also excellent hotel accommodation at the Volcano.

## A TRIP TO HAWAII.

It is the close of day, and of a long day in a hard saddle; I am literally famishing, and my mule is already up to his ears in water cress; but I have ridden, and he has carried me—How just, O Mother Nature, are thy judgments!

With the superb poses of a trained athlete, my native swings a fowl by the neck, and very shortly it is plucked and potted, together with certain vegetables of the proper affinities. Then he swathes a fish in succulent leaves, and buries it in hot ashes; and then he smokes his peace-pipe. Pipe no sooner lighted, than mouths mysteriously gather—five, ten, a dozen of them, magically assemble at the smell of smoke, and take their turn at the curled shell, with a hollow stalk for a mouth-piece.

Dinner at last. O, fish, fruit, and fowl on a mat, on a floor, in a grass hut at evening! How excellent are these—Amen.

Night; supper over; some one twanging upon a stringed instrument of rude native origin. Gossip lags, but darkness and silence and a cigarette are agreeable substitutes.

My native rises haughtily, and lights a lamp that looks very like a diminutive coffee pot with a great flame in the nose of it; he hangs it against a beam, already blackened with smoke, to the peak of the roof. Again, the peace-pipe sweeps the home circle, and is passed out to the mouths of the neighborhood.

The spirit of repose descends upon us; one by one my dusky fellows roll themselves into mummy-like bundles, and lie in a solemn row along the side of the room, sleeping. I, also, will sleep; a great bark-cloth (kapa) that rattles as if it had received seven starchings, is all mine for a covering. I lie with my eyes to the roof, and count the beams that look like an arbor. What is it I see as large as my thumb, cased in brown armor? A cockroach! a melancholy procession of cockroaches passing from one side of the hut, over the roof, with their backs downward, and descending on the other side by the beams—a hundred of them, or perhaps a thousand—"The cry is 'still they come!'" Ha! put out the coffee pot, for these sights are horrible.

Now I will sleep with my face under the kapa, and in an atmosphere of cocoa-nut oil, relieved at intervals by the sulphurous spurt of a match; I do sleep, and find it in spite of every thing highly refreshing.

## X.

"An ocean planet, rounded by a glory,
The billowy glory of the great Pacific,
Withdrawn in spheres remote of rolling blue.

An island, central, with inferior groupings,
Like Jupiter, in the cerulean distance,
Magnificent among his circling moons.

    \*    \*    \*

The heavy mango droops, the slim palm towers,
By inter-tropical shores ; gleam silver summits
(Through wind-clouds) Arctic with eternal frost.

Crowned with the vast white dome of Mauna Loa,
Escarpments rich with the pandanus, ravines,
Cascades and rainbows, form thy globular shell.

A hollow globe ; beneath the snow, the verdure,
The ambient ocean, live, primordial fires,
Which have created, dwell—and may destroy.

    \*    \*    \*

Hush ! hence the theme ! 'Tis torrid noon with freshness
On lake and waterfall, soft vowels and laughter
From brown amphibious girls in Eden's guise.

And as I gaze and write, glorious Hawaii !
I see no terror in thy soaring beauty,
Thy sky of lazuli and sapphire sea."

—*William Gibson.*

The Volcano House is situated upon the brink of the crater of Kilauea, 4,440 feet above sea level. The climate at that altitude is very cool and bracing ; the accommodations all that can be expected or desired. Even if one were not to descend

A Trip to Hawaii.

LAVA FLOW—Near Hilo.

Forbes Co., Boston.

into the crater, 900 feet below, he would still be well repaid for the fatigue of his journey, by the glimpse of that lake of fire as seen from the Volcano House at night.

A zig-zag trail about three-quarters of a mile in length, leads from the lip of the crater to the lava beds below. A guide is with us, who, at intervals, strikes the lava with his staff, sounding it as one sounds ice to test its safety, and the lava field looks not unlike an ice field thickly powdered with coal dust.

Where we now pass was once a seething sea of fire; it is a thick crust of congealed lava that supports us, and beneath it is imprisoned the molten mass which at times spouts forth its terrific fountains of fire; in the eruption of 1880, lava streams were jetted hundreds of feet into the air.

All the possible dangers attending the descent into Kilauea are forgotten in the intoxicating excitement that possesses us. The crevasses we leap; the tunnels and blow-holes, through which we look into fiery furnaces seven times heated; the vapors that at intervals envelop us: the hot brink of the lake of living lava, where waves of liquid fire dash upon the shore, and the thin edges of the waves are spun into threads finer than finest silk, and are then wafted away in the breeze; the rumblings and subterraneous commotions that at times seem to threaten total annihilation— all these have no terrors for us while we are in the midst of them. But at night, when the canopy of vapor, that always hangs above that *inferno*, is like a cloud on fire, and perpetual lightnings play upon the surface of the burning lake, we shudder with thinking of the dangers we have passed, and wonder that we were not consumed when we were in the midst of these merciless engines of destruction.

The great crater of Kilauea is nine miles in circumference; in one corner of it is *Halemauman*—the house of everlasting fire. No where else within the knowledge of mankind is there a living crater to be compared with it. Vesuvius and Ætna are certainly unworthy. Moreover, there is no crater which can be entered, by reason of its peculiar conformation, and explored with ease and comparative safety save Kilauea alone. There have been a few narrow escapes, but no accidents, and it is needless to add that no description can give any one an adequate idea of the incomparable splendor of the scene.

The return from Kilauea may be made through other portions of Hawaii, by the steamer *Planter* and others ; an itinerary is not practicable at this moment, but as, by reason of its infinite variety of scenery and climate, the Hawaiian Group is destined to become one of the most popular resorts of the tourist, new ways will be opened, and new prospects brought within the reach of all.

The Hawaiian Islands have been called the gems of the Pacific, and it is true, that those who have once visited them, bring away a memory as flattering as it is unfading, of the most romantic island Kingdom in the world, a solitary group in a serene sea, where the summer is fragrant and perpetual.

> "How very fair they must have seemed,
> When first they darkened on the deep !
> Like all the wandering seaman dreamed,
> When land rose lovely on his sleep.
>
> How many dreams they turned to truth,
> When first they met the sailor's eye ?
> Green with the sweet earth's southern youth,
> And azure with her southern sky.
>
> —*L. E. L.*

A Trip to Hawaii.

LAUHALA AND COCOANUT GROVE.

*Forbes Co., Boston.*

www.ingramcontent.com/pod-product-compliance
Lightning Source LLC
Chambersburg PA
CBHW020233090426
42735CB00010B/1670